"Discipline will take you where motivation can't."

"Don't be afraid of slow progress,
be afraid of no progress."

100 QUOTES THAT WILL CHANGE YOUR LIFE

"Remember, eagles fly alone,
while sheep flock together."

"There's always a right time
to do the right thing."

"Your path is harder because
your goals are bigger."

"A positive person is someone
you can send to hell and
he will return happy, rested,
tanned and with a thousand
pictures."

"Pain doesn't harm you;
pain builds you."

"Success is the best
kind of revenge."

"The quieter you become,
the more you are able to hear."

"People are like weather. They change every day, but successful people are like the earth, which never changes."

"We all encounter bumps
on the road we travel,
but that doesn't mean
we're on the wrong path."

"When everyone is laughing,
don't do it.
Let them know
you're dangerous among them."

"True comfort is only
appreciated after real effort."

"Don't go back to the past,
don't run to the future;
live here and now."

"Make yourself such a person
that when someone
has a problem with you,
one look is enough and
you will win"

Friends defend you publicly and improve you privately."

"Silence speaks better than words."

Desire is the starting point of all achievements."

"By maintaining calm
during an argument,
you become dangerous."

"Life is not easy,
but you can make it so."

"Man needs his difficulties
because they are necessary
to enjoy success."

"Life is short.
Live as if you were to die today."

"Your goal should be to be exceptional among a group of exceptional people."

If you feel burnt out, remember
that phoenixes rise from ashes."

"A wise person can learn
from their enemies."

"You truly grow when you're out of your comfort zone."

"Being second means
being the first to lose."

"Never be a bandage for someone else's wounds. After they heal, the bandage is always discarded."

"Every failure is an opportunity
to try again, but smarter."

"One bad chapter in a book
doesn't mean
the whole book is bad."

"Focus on yourself and your goal
When you do that
other opinions won't affect you.

"The crazy one is the one who can't control themselves but wants to control others."

"You recognize a true friend
in uncertain times."

The world breaks everyone and afterward
some are strong at the broken places."

"One day someone will break you so much that you'll become unbreakable."

"From one tree, you can
make a thousand matches
but one match can burn
a thousand trees."

"The most challenging part
is deciding to act.
The rest is
a matter of persistence."

"A king needs
a kingdom to be a king,
not a queen."

"Don't be sad when
someone ignores or rejects you.
People usually ignore
precious things because
they can't afford them."

"Sunny days wouldn't
be appreciated without
rainy ones."

"Never lose faith because
when the sun sets,
the stars are still in the sky."

"Never look back unless
you're planning to go that way."

"It's not people who rule us
but our weaknesses.

"Don't go where the path leads;
instead, go where there is
no path and leave a trail."

"Living in your comfort zone
threatens your potential."

"It's better not to start than
to start and not finish."

"One day you'll look back and
realize that what you lost
doesn't compare to
what you gained."

"A person's strength isn't shown by never falling but by being able to rise."

"The biggest mistake you can make in life is fearing that you'll make one."

"Work harder on yourself
than on your job."

"The only thing you can control is
yourself."

"Those who don't learn from
the past
they are doomed to repeat it."

"Every problem has a solution;
if there's no solution,
it's not a problem."

"If the plan doesn't work,
change it,
but never give up on it."

"Don't be afraid to stand out
from the crowd;
the sun never asks
for permission to shine."

"Age doesn't indicate maturity.
Grades don't reflect intelligence.
Gossip doesn't define
who you are."

"Life is a game of poker.
You can't control the cards
you're dealt,
but you can control how
you play your hand."

"Success is not just
the destination but
a demanding journey."

"To become who you want to be
you must sacrifice who you are.

'Be like hell, unconquerable art"

"Don't let the same snake
bite you twice."

"Doubt has killed more dreams
than failure."

"Your thoughts create your
reality."

"The greatest art is
to go through hell and
not become a devil."

"Fear allows a person to reach their highest potential."

"Be the reason your name is remembered."

"When you're happy,
you listen to music;
when you're sad, you start to
understand the lyrics.

"Life is like a piano;
white keys represent success,
black keys represent failure,
but you need both
to play the music."

"Remember, if you shoot just to shoot, you'll never hit, but if you aim, your chances significantly increase."

"Don't cry over what
doesn't cry over you.

"No one wants to see you at the top."

"If you risk nothing,
you risk everything."

"Success isn't for the chosen few
but for those who choose it."

"Live today because yesterday won't return and tomorrow may not come."

"Your past mistakes don't define
who you are."

"While you're busy doubting
yourself,
others are scared of your
potential."

"Your struggle is part of your story."

"Let them talk;
that's all they can do."

"Today you're building the future
not what you'll do tomorrow."

"Keep it private.
People like to ruin things."

"Finding friends is like fishing.
You must offer something first to
catch them."

"Pain leaves you once
it stops teaching you."

"Don't compare yourself
to others;
compare yourself to who
you were yesterday."

"The moment you give up
s the moment you let someone
else wins."

"The road to success
works like an elevator;
on some floors,
you have to leave some
people behind."

"No one is coming to save you;
be your own hero."

"Don't tell them your plans;
show them your results."

"The brain starts working
when the heart breaks."

"No one is stronger than
the person who healed
themselves."

"As long as you're fighting,
you're a winner."

"Remember, a winner is a loser who tried one more time."

"If you lose motivation, remind
yourself why you started."

"If you can dream it,
you can achieve it."

"Win in silence.
A lion doesn't roar after a kill."

"Things must go wrong to
go right."

"Failures teach us much more
than victories."

"Opportunities are not given;
you create them."

"Have your own rules and
your own path."

"Achieve the impossible and you'll stop doubting yourself."

"It's not shameful to lose;
it's shameful not to fight."

www.ingramcontent.com/pod-product-compliance
Lightning Source LLC
Chambersburg PA
CBHW070837260726
48660CB00005B/2066